Moving

By Janine Amos
Photographs by Howard Davies

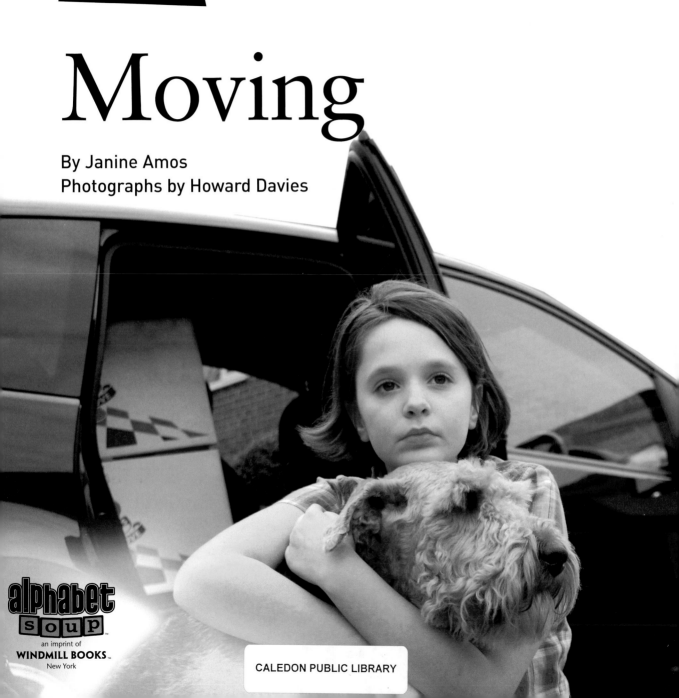

alphabet soup
an imprint of
WINDMILL BOOKS
New York

Published in the United States by Alphabet Soup, an imprint of Windmill Books, LLC

Windmill Books
303 Park Avenue South
Suite #1280
New York, NY 10010

U.S. publication copyright © 2010 Evans Brothers Limited
First North American Edition

Library of Congress Cataloging-in-Publication Data

Amos, Janine
        Moving. – 1st North American ed. / by Janine Amos ; photographs by Howard Davies.
cm. – (Changes)
        Includes bibliographical references and index.
        Summary: Letters, stories, and informational text help children cope
with moving to a new home.
        ISBN 978-1-60754-487-6 (lib.) – ISBN 978-1-60754-488-3 (pbk.)
ISBN 978-1-60754-489-0 (6-pack)
        1. Moving, Household—Juvenile literature   2. Moving, Household—
Psychological aspects—Juvenile literature   3. Moving, Household—Social aspects—
Juvenile literature   [1. Moving, Household]   I. Davies, Howard   II. Title
III. Series
        648/.9—dc22

Manufactured in China

With thanks to our models: Ronald Shaw, Maisie Frost, Finn and Joe Davies, Tai Harrison-Schulz, Rebecca
Natali, Jane and Kim Shaw, Phil Frost, Pickle, Antonia Mann, Sally Hindle and Fenstanton Primary School,
Craig Price, Ann-Marie Buchanan, Leon Labadie, Dionne Arthur-Deneth, Kerry Blakemore, Frederick Afrifa,
Maria Parkes, Amber Bunter, Luke Goozee, Ronnie and David Dewey, Jake Harvey.

Special thanks to the following for all their help: Ruth Marchant at Triangle Services, Chris Smith at
Adventure Unlimited and Bishop's Move.

Contents

Dear Grandpa,

We're moving. Mom and Dad told me yesterday and we went to see the new house. I like my room there but it's much smaller than my old one. All the rooms are smaller. There was a lady there with all her furniture and curtains. She'll move out and we'll move in with our things. I'll have to go to a different school. I'll really miss my friends. And I won't be able to go to Art Club any more. I like Art Club. Everybody knows me there. No one will know me at the new place — it's miles away. We've got to go because Dad couldn't get a job around here. Mom and Dad have known for a long time, but they didn't tell me. They said Finn can come to stay sometimes.

I hope your leg is better.

Love Tom

Dear Tom,

What an exciting letter! Thank you for telling me your news about moving. It sounds like you're feeling a bit mixed up about it all. Half excited and half sad to be leaving? I felt like that when I moved here.

You're bound to miss your old friends. You can write to them and meet up during school vacations. Don't forget, you'll be busy making new friends, too. I know how much you enjoy Art Club. Are you sure there isn't something like it in the new place? Perhaps your mom or dad could help you to find out.

My leg is feeling much better now, and the bandage is off.

Write soon.

Love, Grandpa

Holly and Pickle

"We're moving! We're moving!" sang Holly's little brother Jack. He was jumping in and out of all the boxes in their bedroom. Holly sat on the bed and looked out of the window. She was tired of Jack's silly song. He was only five. To him, everything was a game.

"Come on, Holly," said her dad in a grumpy voice. "You're supposed to be packing your toys — not daydreaming!"

Holly sighed. She kicked one of the boxes with her shoe — but softly, so her dad didn't see. Then she slowly began to fill up the box.

Before Holly went to bed, her dad came to say goodnight. He looked at all the neatly packed boxes and smiled.

"Well done, Holly," he said. "This is the worst part of moving, all this packing. Just wait until we get to the new place! You'll have a big yard to play in — and a room of your own. You'll love it!"

Holly just nodded. When her dad had gone, she went to the window and looked at the yard outside. She could see her old sandpit up against the broken wall. And the patch of ground where she'd done her first headstand. Pickle, their dog, lay asleep on the step.

"I don't want to leave this place," thought Holly. "I like it here." She rested her chin on her hand and let out a big sigh.

The next morning, Holly sat on the bench outside. Pickle sat beside her in the sunshine. She slowly stroked the top of his head.

Holly's mom sat down next to them. "I wonder what Pickle will think of the new place?" she said. "It will be really strange for him at first. He's lived here all his life."

"Just like me," said Holly.

"Mmm," her mom went on. "Everything will smell different, won't it? And his bed will be in a strange room. I wonder if he'll take a while to settle in?"

Holly thought about it. "I could help him," she said. "I could talk to him and show him round. He wouldn't be frightened then, would he?"

Holly's mom gave her a big smile. "That's a great idea!" she said. "We'll put you in charge of Pickle. Thanks, Holly."

Soon it was Moving Day. Holly and Pickle sat in the empty bedroom. Through the window, they watched the movers carrying boxes. Everything was loaded into a huge van.

"Goodbye, bedroom," said Holly sadly.

Just then, Holly's mom came in with Pickle's leash. "Let's put Pickle in the car now," she said. "You can put him in."

Holly attached the leash to Pickle's collar and led him out to the car.

At the new house, Holly led Pickle inside. First they went into the kitchen, where Holly showed Pickle the place his bed would go. Pickle sniffed around for a long time. Then Holly led him upstairs, into her new bedroom. She tried to plan where all her things would go.

Then she took Pickle downstairs and out into the big garden.

"Wow!" Holly gasped, as she sat down on the wall. "You're going to love this, Pickle!" Suddenly, everything seemed much better.

Two days later, Holly and Pickle were in the garden, where Holly's mom and Jack were kicking a soccer ball around. Holly was making Pickle practice some tricks when Holly's mom came over and crouched down beside them.

"Do you think Pickle likes it here?" she asked.

"You bet he does," replied Holly. "Just like me!"

Dear Matt,

I'm sad without you. Nothing is the same. I miss talking to you and playing with you after school. Two new boys have moved into your old house, but I haven't met them yet. I bet they can't do sign language and they might not want to try. So I just sort of hang around. I wish the summer vacation were over.

Here's a kit for making airplanes. Mom said it's a moving-in present. I wish we could come to live next to you in your new house. Mom says we can't. But I can come over at fall break to stay, if that's OK with your mom. We can try out my new basketball hoop.

See you,

Jamie

Dear Jamie,

Thanks for the airplane kit. It's wicked! I'm writing this in my new bedroom. It's really cool here. There are fields behind our house for taking Sooty for walks and a big playground too. Mom and Dad are still unpacking. They take a long time to decide where everything goes. I've been exploring. There are some woods at the back that look great, but I'm not allowed in them on my own. Oh well!

I've seen some boys playing soccer on the field up the road. Mom says she'll come with me if I like and show them some signs. Then we can play together. But I don't know if I want to yet. I'll see. You sound fed up. There's a whole week of summer vacation left. Find out what Billy's doing. You could go to the old farm — there's always something going on down there.

Take care,

Matt

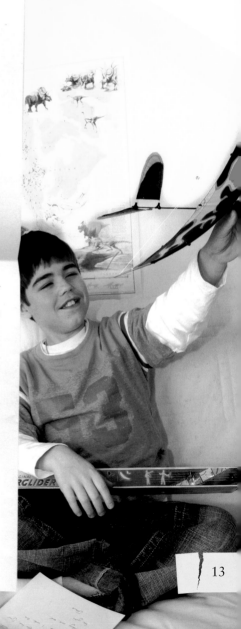

What Will Happen?

When you first hear that you are moving to a new home, you may have lots of questions. How far away will you be going? Will you ne to change schools? What will your new home be like?

■ For many children this is an exciting time. It may be a bit worrying, too. Some children worry that they may not like the new place as much as their old home. It's hard to imagine living somewhere you don't know. Will there be the same things to do? Tom worries that he won't be able to go to Art Club when he moves.

■ Many children feel concerned about fitting in somewhere new. They wonder who they will play with and how they will make friends. The thought of a new school worries lots of children. They wonder if the work will be the same as they are used to. What will the teachers be like?

■ Many children want to know exactly when they will be moving. And their parents find it hard to give an exact date — there may be lots to

sort out. This may make the children feel unsettled.

■ Some children who are moving simply feel sad. Like Tom, they think of the friends they are leaving. For some, this crowds out every other thought.

■ It can be a sad time for those left behind, too. If your best friend is moving away, it can feel like the end of the world for you.

■ It's also a difficult time for parents. There will be a lot of extra work for them. They may seem always busy and impatient. Don't forget, they may be feeling a bit sad, too. They will be leaving behind their own friends and the place they know.

Left Behind

If your best friend is moving away you could make or buy a moving-in present to give them. Fix a time to see them — then you will both have that time to look forward to! If you saw your friend every day at a certain time, plan what you'll do then instead. You might ask another friend over to play, visit someone else, or learn to do something new. Talk about it with your mom or dad.

Getting Ready to Move

If you're feeling sad and confused about moving, don't keep it to yourself. Talk to your mom or dad, or another adult you trust. There are some other ways you can help yourself, too.

■ Find out as much as you can about what is going on. If there's anything practical you are concerned about — such as if you will finish off the year at your old school or where you will be sleeping in the new house — then ask.

■ Ask if you may visit the new place. If not, is there a photograph you could look at? See if you can visit your new school. Look on the bulletin board and find out about after-school clubs and other activities.

■ Plan how you'll arrange your things in your new room. If you'll be sharing a room, think about how you'll arrange it together.

■ Before the move, try to pack up your own things. Then you'll feel in charge. Write your name on the boxes or mark them with stickers. You could leave out one or two special toys and put them in a backpack. Carry this with you on Moving Day.

■ Ask what you can do to help on Moving Day. Like Holly in the story, you might be in charge of the family pet or a younger brother or sister. Talk about it with your parents first.

■ Set up a date for your best friend to visit you in your new home. (Check with your parents first.) Plan to write to your friends. Ask if you may telephone them, too, sometimes.

■ Remember, you will make new friends in your new home, too. We make friends everywhere we go in life. The number of our friends just keeps on growing.

Dear Grandpa,

This is your first letter from our new house! I've just finished unpacking all my things. It took two whole days. The first night here was weird. It was hard to get to sleep. There were all sorts of strange noises. Mom said it was the oil burner. I don't think I'll ever find my way around here. All the streets look exactly the same.

I haven't started my new school yet, but I've been there to visit. One boy in my class was really friendly. His name is Jake.

Finn's coming to stay next weekend. Mom says you are coming soon. I can't wait to show you everything. These are the things I like about here — my room, the street (but there are no trees), the park, Jake at school and the kitchen (but it's full of books). Things I miss — Finn, our old garden, Art Club, my old school and my teacher.

See you soon,

Love, Tom

Dear Tom,

Thank you for your letter. I'm really looking forward to my visit.

I'm glad that the move went well. It will take some time for you all to settle in. I remember it took me a while to feel that this was my home, and I only moved from two streets away! Once you've started at school, you'll soon get to know people. I think you need to do lots of things in your house to make it feel yours. How about having some school friends over after school?

Why don't you make a map of your new neighborhood? Ask Mom or Dad to go for a walk with you over the weekend. Make a note of all the landmarks as you go along — stores, mailboxes, traffic lights, churches, and trees. When you get home, draw it out on a big sheet of paper. That will help you find your way around. It will also help me avoid getting lost when I come to stay!

Love, Grandpa

In a New Place

For many children, learning to enjoy a new place takes hardly any time. They find they've made themselves at home almost right away. For others, settling in takes longer.

■ Some children hate the feeling of being new. They don't know what to do with themselves after school. They aren't sure of their way around. They stay at home a lot. This may make them feel lonely or bored.

■ Other children feel worried about what each new day will bring. They take it out on people at home. They snap at others or become moody.

■ Some children take longer to fit into a new school than others. They keep thinking of the way they used to do things in their old school. Everything in the new school can seem different and confusing.

■ Some children find it hard to make new friends. They worry about what others are thinking of them. They feel shy and left out.

■ Many children who have moved feel extra tired at the end of the day. Remembering new names and places is tiring for anyone. It's a good idea to get plenty of rest.

■ If you feel any of these things, don't worry. They are all part of being new. Do try telling someone — a parent or another adult you trust. It would help to tell your teacher, too. He or she may have some other ideas for helping you to settle in.

■ Remember that life changes all the time. And mostly change brings new and good things.

Pets on the Move

Moving to a new home can be a confusing for your pets, too. Everywhere looks and smells different. If you have a cat, keep it indoors for the first few days. Introduce your pet to one room first, let it sniff around and feel safe. Slowly let it explore the whole house. Always feed your pet in the same place. Just like people, some animals take longer than others to settle in. Give them time — and plenty of affection.

Give It Time

If you are finding it hard to settle in to life in the new place, it might help to remember these things:

■ Learning the way around your new area will give you confidence. Look at a map and talk it through with a grown-up. Make your own map, as Tom's grandpa suggested.

■ Never be afraid to ask. If there's something you don't understand at your new school — like a new way of doing things, or where a room is — ask someone.

■ If you're feeling lonely and left out, think what you can do to change things. Make a list of all the places you could go to meet others — gym club, the sports center, swimming club, the park. Ask an adult to help you. Is there anyone at school you'd like to invite to your home?

■ Other people don't know what you're thinking. If you keep to yourself, people may not realize that you're just feeling shy. They may think you are unfriendly. Be brave and greet people with a smile! It may seem hard at first — but practice helps.

■ Give yourself time. It takes a while to get to know new people. Try not to be too upset if one group doesn't seem friendly. Keep trying. There's someone out there who would love to be your friend.

Making Friends

Here are some ideas to help when you're feeling shy. Think about the other person. Try to forget about yourself — just for a moment. Smile and say, "Hello." (Your heart might beat faster and you might go red. Try not to worry — it's normal to feel like this sometimes.) Ask the other person a question about themselves. This shows the other person that you care. And you'll learn something about them.

Luke's New School

Luke tried to eat the toast in front of him, but his throat was too dry to swallow.

"All ready?" asked Luke's mom, coming into the kitchen. "We'd better get going soon. We don't want to be late on your first day!" Luke's heart started to thump in his chest.

As his mom locked the door behind them, Luke could feel his heart beating faster. He was nervous. It was his first day in his new school.

As Luke walked beside his mom, the streets filled with children. They walked in groups or in pairs, laughing and talking together.

"I wonder if any of those kids will be in my class?" thought Luke.

"I'll wait here and make sure you make it inside," said Luke's mom at the gates.

"OK," nodded Luke, gratefully.

In the classroom, Mr. Michael, the teacher, introduced Luke to the class. There was a new girl, too, named Emma.

"I'm sure everyone's excited to get to know you both," said Mr. Michael, smiling.

Luke's cheeks burned with embarassment. He looked down at his feet. Emma looked as though she was feeling the same.

It was the start of a new school year. Mr. Michael handed out books and explained where everything was. Luke tried to concentrate, but he wasn't really listening.

"What will happen at recess?" he wondered, panicking. "Who will I talk to? What should I do?"

At last, recess came. The class rushed out into the playground. Luke stood by himself, feeling awkward. He wished he could go home right now.

A boy came by. Luke recognized him from his class. His name was Daniel. He smiled at Luke and said "Hello." But Luke couldn't say a word. He nodded and quickly put his head down.

Daniel walked away. Luke stayed where he was. He pretended he didn't care. But inside he wanted to cry.

Daniel and the others started running around. They were playing some kind of chase game. Luke watched them out of the corner of his eye.

Just then, Daniel suddenly collapsed on to the ground and started to shake. The others stopped. They stood and stared, not knowing what to do.

Without thinking, Luke picked up a coat and dashed over to Daniel. He remembered what he had done when his cousin had an epileptic fit. Luke put the coat under Daniel's head, loosened his collar, and waited until he had stopped shaking. Then he turned him on his side, into the recovery position. The other children came closer and watched with amazement.

By the time Mr. Michael arrived, Daniel had opened his eyes.

"Are you OK, Daniel?" Mr. Michael asked, crouching down beside him. "That must have been a shock."

Mr. Michael looked at Luke.

"Well done, Luke," he said. "You did exactly the right thing and kept Daniel from hurting himself."

After a rest in the principal's office, Daniel joined the others in class. He smiled across at Luke, and Luke smiled back.

At lunchtime, Luke sat with Daniel and a girl named Sue.

"We thought you were really stuck up at first," said Daniel.

Sue nodded. "You wouldn't look at us or say hello."

"I was shy, that's all," explained Luke. "It's hard being new."

"Well, you're not new anymore," said Daniel, laughing. "It feels as if I've known you forever."

And Luke knew exactly what he meant.

Dear Matt,

We've got Mrs. Fielding this term — she's great. We're doing special projects about where we live and what it used to be like hundreds of years ago. What's your new school like?

I hang out with Josh and Callum now. We go to the park after school — you know the part where we made a den? It's Callum's birthday on Saturday. He's having a swimming party with pizza afterward at his house. It'll be great. There's a new boy Joe in class this year. He's OK. I'm going to his house on Wednesday. We do judo after school on Wednesdays. I told you I was starting. Do they have judo at your school?

See you in two weeks (during the break).

Jamie

Dear Jamie

It's great here. Wait till you see it! We play soccer every day. There's a boy Sam, and he's got a big brother named Patrick. On weekends we pack up sandwiches for lunch. We eat them in the field like a picnic. We can do it when you come.

I like school, too. Our teacher is Mr. Nicol. He wears glasses and looks serious, but he's a real joker. We have more homework than at Westley Park, but it's okay. We aren't allowed to play ball in the playground at school because someone smashed a window last term. We have to go out to the field. It gets all muddy when it rains and we get filthy — Dad hates it! We don't have judo at our school, but I go swimming on Thursdays.

See you next week. Bring your sports clothes!

Bye!

Matt

Glossary

moving (MOO-ving)
Changing the place where a person lives and keeps his or her belongings

moving day (MOO-ving DAY)
The day that a person moves his or her belongings from one place to another place to live

packing (PAK-ing)
To gather belongings into boxes or containers to prepare for a move

shy (SHI)
To be afraid or hesitant to approach or talk to others

worry (WUR-ee)
To feel upset or troubled by certain thoughts or fears

For Further Reading

Thomas, Pat. *Do I Have to Go to the Hospital?: A First Look at Going to the Hospital.* Barron's Educational Series, Inc., 2006.

Civardi, Anne. *Going to the Hospital.* EDC Publishing, 2005.

Web Sites

To find Web sites related to the subject of this book, please go to www.windmillbooks.com/weblinks and select this book's title.

Index

For more great fiction and nonfiction, go to windmillbooks.com.